FINANCING SUSTAINABLE AND RESILIENT FOOD SYSTEMS IN ASIA AND THE PACIFIC

OCTOBER 2021

ADB

ASIAN DEVELOPMENT BANK

© 2021 Asian Development Bank
6 ADB Avenue, Mandaluyong City, 1550 Metro Manila, Philippines
Tel +63 2 8632 4444; Fax +63 2 8636 2444
www.adb.org

Some rights reserved. Published in 2021.

ISBN 978-92-9269-129-5 (print), 978-92-9269-130-1 (electronic), 978-92-9269-131-8 (ebook)
Publication Stock No. SPR210428-2
DOI: http://dx.doi.org/10.22617/SPR210428-2

The views expressed in this publication are those of the authors and do not necessarily reflect the views and policies of the Asian Development Bank (ADB) or its Board of Governors or the governments they represent.

ADB does not guarantee the accuracy of the data included in this publication and accepts no responsibility for any consequence of their use. The mention of specific companies or products of manufacturers does not imply that they are endorsed or recommended by ADB in preference to others of a similar nature that are not mentioned.

By making any designation of or reference to a particular territory or geographic area, or by using the term "country" in this document, ADB does not intend to make any judgments as to the legal or other status of any territory or area.

Please contact pubsmarketing@adb.org if you have questions or comments with respect to content, or if you wish to obtain copyright permission for your intended use that does not fall within these terms, or for permission to use the ADB logo.

Corrigenda to ADB publications may be found at http://www.adb.org/publications/corrigenda.

Notes:
In this publication, "$" refers to United States dollars.
ADB recognizes "China" as the People's Republic of China.

On the cover: **Bountiful harvest.** Workers plucking chilies from the fields at Gabbur, Raichur district, Karnataka, India (photo by ADB).

Contents

Figures and Boxes

Foreword

The coronavirus disease (COVID-19) pandemic has disrupted economic growth and increased the threat to food and nutritional security among vulnerable households in Asia and the Pacific. One of the most important lessons that we learned from this pandemic is the vulnerability of our food supply chains. Weak logistics and storage systems exacerbated the disruption of food supply chains that arose from preventive measures during the pandemic. The proximity of humans and animals in wet markets in the region is increasing the risk of new or reemerging zoonotic diseases. Unsustainable agricultural practices in our region pose serious threats to long-term food security. Balancing the health of people, animals, and the environment is crucial for sustainable and resilient recovery from the pandemic.

All these lessons increase the urgency of building sustainable and resilient food systems. Despite large investment needs in food system transformation, the region is facing a number of constraints to closing the financing gap. We need to effectively mobilize public and private finance through reorientation of public finance and policy institutions, as well as scaling up private investment in food system transformation. We also need to leverage the rapid embrace of digital technology in generating new businesses and financial models that can help accelerate food system transformation.

This report, *Financing Sustainable and Resilient Food Systems in Asia and the Pacific*, reviews the challenges in food system transformation in the region and discusses ways to close the large financing gap through public and private actions. The report recommends actions for the Asian Development Bank (ADB) to support sustainable and resilient transformation of food systems in Asia and the Pacific, leveraging the bank's knowledge capacity and financial instruments.

ADB, through Strategy 2030, is providing investments and technical assistance to promote rural development and food security as well as to enhance environmental sustainability and climate resilience in its developing member countries (DMCs). Moving forward, ADB's support is required for more integrated solutions taking into consideration the interconnected economic, social, and environmental dimensions of food supply chains. Building a strong knowledge base is the first step toward achieving this strategic goal.

This year is an opportune time to discuss the transformation of food systems given the major global event in September, the UN Food Systems Summit, and a biannual event, the ADB Rural Development and Food Security Forum 2021. I am pleased to introduce this report to governments, development partners, the private sector, and civil society in ADB DMCs to advance the policy discussion in the region. I sincerely hope that the knowledge, experiences, lessons learned, and recommendations presented here can inspire innovative thinking and collaboration to accelerate sustainable and resilient transformation of food systems in Asia and the Pacific.

Bruno Carrasco
Director General concurrently Chief Compliance Officer
Sustainable Development and Climate Change Department
Asian Development Bank

Acknowledgments

This report was prepared by the team led by Shingo Kimura (senior natural resources and agriculture specialist, East Asia Department, ADB), Kevin Chen (Qushi chair professor and international dean, China Academy for Rural Development, Zhejiang University and senior research fellow and head of East and Central Asia Office, International Food Policy Research Institute), and Qingfeng Zhang (chief of ADB's Rural Development and Food Security Thematic Group). Mariel A. Gabriel (consultant) provided copyediting support while Rodel I. Valenzuela (consultant) did the layout and typesetting. Administrative support was provided by Leah Arboleda (natural resources and agriculture officer, Rural Development and Food Security Thematic Group) and Erin Lumanta-Sea (associate operations analyst, Rural Development and Food Security Thematic Group).

An earlier draft of this report was peer-reviewed by Jessica Fanzo (Bloomberg Distinguished Professor of Global Food Policy and Ethics at the Johns Hopkins University), Shenggen Fan (dean, Academy of Global Food Economics and Policy and chair professor, College of Economics and Management, China Agricultural University), and Lars Hein (professor Ecosystem Services and Environmental Change and deputy chair of the Environmental Systems Analysis Group, Wageningen University). Yue Zhan (research analyst, East and Central Asia Office, International Food Policy Research Institute) provided research assistance.

Special thanks are extended to the participants in the ADB Sustainable Food Webinar Series on Financing Sustainable and Resilient Food Systems on 16 March 2021, and ADB peer reviewers.

Abbreviations

ADB	Asian Development Bank
COVID 19	coronavirus disease
EDF	Environmental Defense Fund
EU	European Union
FAO	Food and Agriculture Organization of the United Nations
GHG	greenhouse gas
PRC	People's Republic of China
SMEs	small and medium-sized enterprises

Introduction

Asia and the Pacific continues to face nutritional challenges, despite considerable progress in agricultural production, poverty reduction, and food security.[1] It accounts for 58% of the undernourished population globally and in many countries in the region people suffer from one or more forms of malnutrition (Food and Agriculture Organization of the United Nations [FAO] 2020a). The prevalence of stunting and wasting in the region remains high, with stunting rates exceeding 22% in most of the countries. As of 2018, an estimated 82 million children under 5 years of age in the region were stunted, and 34 million suffered from wasting. On the other hand, an estimated 15.7 million children under 5 years of age were considered overweight in 2018. The prevalence of overweight and obesity in both adults and school-age children is rising more rapidly in Asia and the Pacific than any other region, and increasing the associated health care cost (United Nations Economic and Social Commission for Asia and the Pacific 2020). In many countries, leading causes of overweight and obesity are increasingly sedentary lifestyles, rapid urbanization, changing modes of transportation, and increased intake of foods that are high in fats, salt, and sugar.[2] Child undernutrition, overweight, obesity, and micronutrient deficiencies are converging at the national level and in individual households, calling for a cross-sectoral approach to address these issues (FAO et al. 2019).

The coronavirus disease (COVID-19) pandemic increased this food and nutrition security risk. According to Asian Development Bank (ADB) estimates, between 90 million and 400 million people in Asia and the Pacific could fall back into poverty during the pandemic (ADB 2020). The COVID-19 pandemic increased food insecurity risks and deteriorated nutritional status of vulnerable populations due to rising unemployment, reduced remittance, restrictions on people's movement, interruptions in food production and processing, disruptions to supply chains, and increasing international commodity prices. According to the World Food Programme, the number of people who are facing acute food insecurity will nearly double to 265 million by the end of 2020 globally. Lack of action in response to COVID-19 will leave deep impacts on early-life nutrition with possible intergenerational consequences for child growth and development, life-long impacts on education, chronic disease risks, and overall human capital formation (FAO et al. 2021).

The COVID-19 pandemic highlighted the fragility of food supply chains, such as in many developing countries where weak logistics and storage systems exacerbated the disruption

---

[1]   In this this report, Asia and the Pacific indicates developing member countries of ADB.

[2]   McKinsey Global Institute (2014) estimated that obesity has an economic impact of about $2 trillion, or 2.8% of global gross domestic product based on "disability-adjusted life years."

to production and distribution including food loss and waste, food safety, both under- and overnutrition, supply and/or demand balance, and inequality of access (Fan et al. 2021). More frequent extreme weather events associated with climate change are increasing the vulnerability of agricultural production. The public health risk associated with food supply chains also became apparent, calling for One Health—a collaborative, multisector, and transdisciplinary approach to ensure human, animal, and environmental health. The World Health Organization estimates that at least 61% of infectious diseases are zoonotic and originate from animals and have represented 75% of all the emerging infectious disease during the past decade such as severe acute respiratory syndrome and highly pathogenic avian influenza. In Asia and the Pacific, the proximity between humans and animals in wet markets is considered to be the root cause of the exchange of pathogens and enables the potential outbreak of new zoonotic diseases.

These risks and fragilities have added to the issues already facing the sector, where food supply chains account for a major part of the climate and environmental footprint. Agriculture is the largest consumer of the world's freshwater resources and more than one-quarter of the energy used globally is expended on food production and distribution. Agricultural production in Asia and the Pacific grew rapidly due to new technologies, mechanization, increased chemical use, and policies and subsidies that focused on boosting food production. However, conventional agricultural production systems revealed many negative effects such as soil erosion; reduced soil fertility and health; overexploited water resources; increased water, soil, and plastic pollution; deforestation; biodiversity loss; and food safety and human health risks.[3] Food supply chains contribute up to 29% of greenhouse gas (GHG) emissions, including 44% of methane (Intergovernmental Panel on Climate Change 2020).[4] The extension of agricultural land also results in carbon releases due to deforestation or the destruction of other types of ecosystems such as peatland or savannah. There is a clear need across the region to shift from a focus on singular food production and intensification to one that integrates additional aspects of value chain development, sustainable natural resource management, nutrient-rich diets, and public health; and enhances resilience and mitigates climate change.

Food is a common thread linking multiple development challenges, given the interconnected economic, social, and environmental dimensions of food systems. Beyond its direct linkage with United Nations Sustainable Development Goal 2 on achieving zero hunger, food links all 17 Sustainable Development Goal. Food systems gather all the elements (e.g., environment, people, inputs, processes, infrastructures,

---

[3]   The report by the Intergovernmental Science-Policy Platform on Biodiversity and Ecosystem Services (2019) shows that 1 million species are now threatened with extinction, posing serious threats for humans. Agriculture is responsible for up to 80% of biodiversity loss and continues to overuse scarce natural resources including water, forests, and land. The pressures that food production has put on natural resources have left 25% of the world's cultivated land area degraded. These nonmarketed costs—through their impact on health, nutrition, and the natural environment—have been estimated to cost $12 trillion a year, compared with a market value of the global food system of $10 trillion (Food and Land Use Coalition 2019).

[4]   It includes all the elements (environment, people, inputs, processes, infrastructures, institutions, etc.) and activities that relate to the production, processing, distribution, preparation, and consumption of food, and the output of these activities, including socioeconomic and environmental outcomes at the global level. (Intergovernmental Panel on Climate Change 2020).

and institutions) and activities that relate to the production, processing, distribution, preparation, and consumption of food, and the outputs of these activities, including socioeconomic, health, and environmental outcomes (FAO-UN Environment 2014). A food system approach can provide integrated solutions, taking into account the interrelationships among its elements.[5] Building sustainable and resilient food systems would address major development challenges in the region and provide an opportunity for ADB to achieve its operational priorities of Strategy 2030 (Box 1).

Box 1: What Are Sustainable and Resilient Food Systems?

As defined by the United Nations, sustainability is "meeting the needs of the present without compromising the ability of future generations to meet their own needs" (World Commission on Environment and Development 1987). Sustainability has basic goals to support environmental and population health, economic profitability, and social equity; in other words, it is balancing people, planet, and profits. In the food system context, sustainability refers to the long-term viability of current food systems and how they interact with and manage the natural and human resources upon which they rely to provide people with livelihood so that they contribute to a robust economy.

Resilience is a crucial complementary and integrated feature of sustainable food systems, given the multiple risks to the systems. The Organisation for Economic Co-operation and Development (2020a) defines resilience as the ability of individuals, households, communities, cities, institutions, systems, and societies to prevent, resist, absorb, adapt, respond, and recover positively, efficiently, and effectively when faced with a wide range of risks, while maintaining an acceptable level of functioning and without compromising long-term prospects for sustainable development, peace and security, human rights, and well-being for all. A resilient food system would have abilities to (i) respond to and cope with an adverse event in the short term, (ii) make incremental changes in response to current or expected future circumstances, and (iii) create a fundamentally new system when ecological, economic, or social structures make the existing system untenable. As the shocks affect the most vulnerable and food-insecure in greater measure, policies should improve access to knowledge, technologies, and services for those most at risk, as well as enhance institutional and technical capacities at all levels to deliver disaster risk reduction.

Beyond supplying safe and nutritious food to consumers, sustainable and resilient food systems would improve environmental and population health, economic viability, and social equity and, therefore, contribute to the achievement of Asian Development Bank's seven operational priorities.

Source: Organisation for Economic Co-operation and Development (OECD). 2020. *Strengthening Agricultural Resilience in the Face of Multiple Risks*. Paris: OECD Publishing.

---

[5]   In this report, the scope of food systems includes supply chains of fiber and other plants or animal products.

Sustainable and Resilient Food Systems and ADB's Operational Priorities

Poverty Gender Climate Resilience and Environment Livable Cities Food Security and Rural Development Governance Regional Cooperation

Food Systems

Employment *Ecosystem services* *Water pollution* *GHG emissions* *Nutrition and health* *Food safety* *Trade*

Food supply chain

Food production and input supply → Processing and packaging → Retail and marketing → Consumers

Sustainable and Resilient Transformation

- Sustainable production practice
- Regenerative farming
- Integration of smallholders with value chains

- Use of renewable biological resources
- Sustainable protein solutions

- Resilient logistics and food reserve systems
- Strengthening biosecurity to prevent zoonotic disease

- Access to healthy and nutritious diet
- Consumption choice based on environmental and climate footprint

GHG = greenhouse gas.
Source: Asian Development Bank.

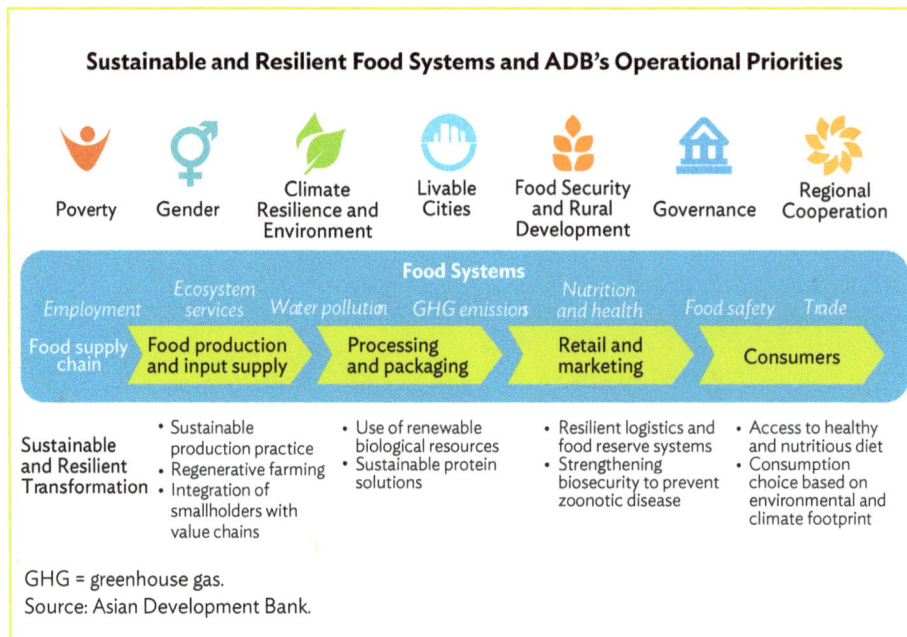

However, financing is a major challenge in the sustainable and resilient transformation of food systems. As the recovery from the COVID-19 pandemic presents an opportunity to build sustainable and resilient food systems, public and private actors need to consider the risk landscape over the long term, and place a greater emphasis on what can be done in advance to reduce risk exposure and increase preparedness. While this requires significant investment both from the public and private sectors, there are a number of constraints to scaling up financing for food system transformation. The main purpose of this report is to discuss how to close the large financing gap in food system transformation in Asia and the Pacific through reforms in public finance and policy institutions, making use of financial instruments and mechanisms to channel private investment, and leveraging digital technologies. The report also proposes possible actions for ADB to help develop sustainable and resilient food systems in Asia and the Pacific.

Food System Approach as an Instrument to Address Major Development Challenges in Asia and the Pacific

Ending Hunger and Malnutrition

Increasing the accessibility, affordability, and availability of safe and nutritious foods is the main responsibility of food systems. First, the quantity and diversity of nutrient-rich foods should be increased through sustainable and resilient farming. Second, nutrients generated in the food system need to be retained to ensure accessibility to sustainable and healthy diets. Approximately one-third of all food produced is lost or wasted globally (FAO 2011). Significant scope exists to reduce food loss and waste by setting actionable targets, promoting affordable household-level, food-storage technologies, and making use of innovative technologies such as dehydration, low-cost solar drying, microcold transport, biodegradable coatings, and traceability. Reducing waste throughout food supply chains reduces the need for food production and reduces the pressure for higher yields to meet food security goals. Third, increasing purchasing power is fundamental to the goal of making sustainable, healthy diets affordable to all. Improved knowledge of the environmental and health implications of food choices, and carefully designed consumer-level taxes and subsidies can help make staples and nutrient-rich foods more affordable to more people.

Climate Resilience and Environmental Sustainability

Several countries in Asia, including the People's Republic of China (PRC), Japan, and the Republic of Korea, have announced the ambitious target for carbon neutrality by the mid-21st century. At the food production stage, improving efficiency in the use of inputs through sustainable intensification can help reduce carbon footprint. Management measures exist to significantly reduce the GHG emissions from agricultural production sources, particularly enteric fermentation by ruminants, manure, nitrogen fertilizers, and energy use (Box 2). At the retail level, the use of refrigeration and refrigerant leakage from refrigerators and freezers has been identified as a substantial contributor to direct GHG emissions from supermarkets (FAO). Reducing refrigerant leakage and improving energy use in the retailing, marketing, and distribution of food are examples of potential mitigation measures that can be applied in the postharvest stages of the food supply chains. A notable policy

> ### Box 2: Environmental and Public Health Linkages of Livestock Sector
>
> Increasing incomes, changing diets, and population growth have shifted toward more consumption of animal protein. As a result, the livestock sector became one of the fastest growing agricultural subsectors in Asia. This represents a major opportunity for smallholders, agribusiness, and job creators throughout the livestock supply chain. However, the livestock sector represents 14.5% of all human-induced greenhouse gas emissions, in which ruminants account for more than 80% of the total livestock emission (Herrero et al. 2013). The manure emission from intensive livestock production, if not properly managed, leads to excessive nitrogen imbalance, which could result in biodiversity loss and pose risks to human health and the eutrophication of surface water. In many countries in the region, overgrazing has been degrading grasslands (Intergovernmental Science-Policy Platform on Biodiversity and Ecosystem Services 2019). While meat provides an important source of nutrition such as protein and vitamins, excessive consumption of red meat and processed meat is known to increase the risk of several cancers (World Health Organization 2015). Increasing meat consumption in the region is a notable area that the integrated food system approach—and its economic, environment, health, and social consequences—is required to address simultaneously.
>
> Sources: Herrero, M. et al. 2013. Biomass Use, Production, Feed Efficiencies, and Greenhouse Gas Emissions from Global Livestock Systems. *Proceedings of the National Academy of Sciences*. 110 (52). pp. 20888–20893; Intergovernmental Science-Policy Platform on Biodiversity and Ecosystem Services (IPBES). 2019. *Summary for policymakers of the regional assessment report on biodiversity and ecosystem services for Asia and the Pacific of the Intergovernmental Science-Policy Platform on Biodiversity and Ecosystem Services.* Bonn: IPBES Secretariat; WHO. 2015. Cancer: Carcinogenicity of the Consumption of Red Meat and Processed Meat.

example taking a whole supply chain approach is the Farm-to-Fork Strategy of the European Union (EU) announced in May 2020, as part of the EU's Green Deal policy initiative to achieve carbon neutrality by 2050.[6]

Integrated Rural Development

Food systems provide incomes and livelihoods to farmers and many others in the economy. Many rural service sectors connected to food supply chains are provided locally. Food systems are a dominant user of natural resources in rural areas. A systems

---

[6] The strategy mandates the European Commission to develop a framework for a sustainable food system before the end of 2023 to promote policy coherence at the EU and national level, mainstream sustainability in all food-related policies, and strengthen the resilience of food systems. The framework will also address the responsibilities of all actors in the food system. The strategy has 27 concrete actions to transform the EU's food system by 2030, including: (i) 50% reduction in the use and risk of pesticides; (ii) at least 20% reduction in the use of fertilizers, including animal manure; (iii) 50% reduction in sales of antimicrobials used for farm animals and aquaculture; and (iv) an increase in agricultural land for organic farming from 8% to 25%. As next steps, the European Commission will work on common definitions, general principles, and requirements for sustainable food systems and foods.

approach to adopt more multisectoral solutions linking food security, nutrition, and poverty would improve the desired socioeconomic objective of eliminating poverty, hunger, and malnutrition. Integration of smallholder farmers to value chains generate better economic opportunities in rural areas and improve access to food. A food system approach can support integrated rural development to achieve food and nutrition security, rural poverty reduction and economic growth, and improve social and environmental well-being in rural areas (Figure 1). This requires sound services

Figure 1: Food System Transformation and Integrated Rural Development

1. Food and nutrition security

- Innovative technologies to boost agricultural productivity
- Nutrition-sensitive and adaptive social protection programs
- Increase availability and accessibility of healthy and nutritious diets

2. Rural poverty reduction and economic growth

- Smallholders join food value chains
- Narrow rural and/or urban digital divide
- Structured financing for rural SMEs

3. Social and environmental well-being in rural areas

- Support sustainable agricultural production
- Invest in rural health, education, and social protection system
- Invest in rural environmental infrastructure (e.g., waste management)
- Reduce gender gap
- Finance rural green business (e.g., bio-based industries to establish local circular economy)

SMEs = small and medium-sized enterprises.
Source: Asian Development Bank.

in place, including basic social services, improvement of the local environment, and rural–urban integration to build on market opportunities. The evolution of rural development policies in the PRC showcases the shift to an integrated rural development to improve social, economic, and environmental welfare.[7]

Moving forward, the integrated model of rural development needs to ensure sustainable and resilient transformation of food systems is economically viable, achieving environmental sustainability and food security and economic prosperity simultaneously. One key option to remove carbon dioxide from the atmosphere lies in the linkage between agriculture and forestry, notably through afforestation and the development of sustainable bioenergies (Organisation for Economic Co-operation and Development [OECD] 2019). A circular bioeconomy is a notable initiative to establish sustainable and resilient food systems at a local scale including forestry and

---

[7] The Rural Vitalization Strategy in the PRC announced in 2017 has taken a wider approach to promoting integrated rural development focusing on poverty reduction through enhancing rural–urban integration, speeding up agriculture modernization, promoting ecological protection, enhancing the rural environment and villages, and providing basic services including rural wastewater and sanitation.

other biological sectors. Promoting the use of renewal biological resources can covert waste streams into value-added products and contribute to the conversion of natural resources. The EU considers a circular bioeconomy as a key rural initiative to address multiple societal challenges including food security, climate change adaptation, and rural development (Box 3).

Box 3: Bioeconomy Strategy in the European Union

A circular economy concept prioritizes resource efficiency and resilience, and aims to maintain the value of products, materials, and resources for as long as possible by returning them into the product cycle at the end of their use while minimizing the generation of waste (FAO 2020b). A bioeconomy is similar to a circular economy; it encompasses the production of renewable biological resources and the conversion of these resources and waste streams into value-added products such as food, feed, bio-based products, and bioenergy (European Commission 2018).

In 2018, the European Union (EU) announced its updated bioeconomy strategy with five goals: (i) ensuring food and nutrition security; (ii) managing natural resources sustainably; (iii) reducing dependence on nonrenewable, unsustainable resources whether sourced domestically or from abroad; (iv) mitigating and adapting to climate change; and (v) strengthening European competitiveness and creating jobs. The action plan includes 14 concrete actions. Establishing a local bioeconomy and unlocking investments by public and private stakeholders are the main components of each goal. The action plan launched a European Circular Bioeconomy Fund, a venture fund with a target size of €250 million to which the European Investment Bank has committed €100 million.

As a part of the background study for the European Circular Bioeconomy Fund, the European Investment Bank recognized the access to finance issue, in particular scaling up bioeconomy-related investments from pilot to demonstration projects and to flagship and industrial-scale plants. The study found market and demand risks as the highest business risk factor for investments. Filling the financial gap requires an effective, stable, and supportive regulatory framework including coherent biomass certification frameworks in the EU. It also found that push mechanisms, such as grants, are not sufficient in size or catalytic impact and need to be complemented by different public and private sector interventions to fill the financial gaps.

Sources: European Commission. 2018. A Sustainable Bioeconomy for Europe: Strengthening the Connection Between Economy, Society and the Environment – Updated Bioeconomy Strategy. FAO. 2020. Circular Economy: Waste-to-Resource & COVID-19.

Financing is a major challenge for food system transformation. The transformation to sustainable and resilient food systems requires an effective mobilization of public and private finance. FAO, the International Fund for Agricultural Development, and the World Food Programme (2015) estimated that ending poverty and hunger requires additional financing in agriculture and rural development of $140 billion annually. Blended Finance Taskforce (2020) estimated the annual investment requirement for the critical transformation of food and land use systems is between $300 billion to $350 billion by 2030 globally.[8] Scaling up public finance for sustainable and resilient food systems became even more challenging under the increasing fiscal pressures to cope with the economic impacts of the COVID-19 pandemic. Closing a large financing gap would require a reorientation of the finance program and institutional reforms to facilitate the public and private investment in food system transformation.

Reorientation of Public Finance and Policy Institutions

Public finance should be reoriented to sustainable and resilient food systems.
The OECD (2020b) estimates that of $708 billion spent annually to support their agricultural sectors during the 2017–2019 period in 54 countries, two-fifths were provided through policies that artificially maintain domestic farm prices, while another 9% were payments linked to output or the unconstrained use of variable inputs. Subsidies coupled with production often fail to provide consistent incentives to preserve natural capital and support sustainable production. In particular, subsidies for variable production inputs lead to overuse of groundwater, fertilizers, and pesticides. Reallocating the distortive form of support can increase efficiency and free up considerable funds that could be used to support sustainable and resilient food systems. Coherence of farm payments with a sustainability policy objective can be improved through imposing environmental conditions on the receipt of farm payments. The last round of European agricultural reforms made 30% of payments to farmers conditional upon additional conservation measures. Brazil has sought to link subsidized farm credit to forest protection, while increasing the efficient use of land for cattle grazing (World Bank 2018). The risk exposure to catastrophic weather

---

8   Among the required annual investment, almost half of the investment ($150 billion a year) is needed for investment in rural infrastructure, extension services, financing smallholders, education for girls, and family planning. Approximately $100 billion in new investments will be needed in regenerative agriculture practices, to support a healthy and productive oceans, and to restore forests and other critical ecosystems.

events can be mitigated by public support to enhance farmer's capacity to manage risk.

Policy institutions should provide right incentives to take actions to transform food systems. Environmental benefits generated by agricultural conservation practices, including GHG emission reductions, water quality improvements, and biodiversity, remain unpriced externalities (Environmental Defense Fund [EDF] 2020). Farmers have little incentives to pursue sustainable agriculture and the protection of natural assets without incurring significant cost or loss of income in the presence of the disconnection between the retail price of food and the cost of production and distribution reflecting implicit environmental costs. The lack of a market-accepted valuation methodology prevents investors from embedding natural capital and environmental benefits into financing decisions. Policy institutions should provide incentives through regulations, public payments (charges and reduction in levies) to private resource users for the enhancement (or degradation) of ecosystem services; open trading between private resource users under a regulatory cap or floor for the level of use or investment in natural capital; self-organized private deals between the off-site beneficiaries of natural capital and the resource owners; and the ecolabeling and certification of sustainably produced products that consumers are willing to pay a price premium for (Scherr, White, and Kaimowitz 2004). Uncertainty in both the regulatory and market environment can increase stakeholder's risk perception to scale up their investments in sustainable and resilient food systems. Developing a stable and supportive institutional and market environment is critical to promote investment in sustainable and resilient food systems.

(i)   **Environmental regulations.** Environmental performance standards are a common method of regulating polluting emissions from nonagricultural point sources. Environmental performance standards typically impose an upper limit on the externality or the selected indicator (OECD 2010). Performance standards allow polluters to find ways to achieve the standards at minimum cost, which promote cost-saving innovations. On the other hand, input standards place mandates or constraints directly on producers' choices. In agriculture, imposing performance standards is difficult as the emissions are often nonpoint sources. Applying process standards in agriculture is also challenging due to high monitoring costs. Such standards are not effective unless they are adapted to local ecological conditions.

(ii)   **Environmental taxes.** An environmental tax corrects the incentive failures resulting from missing markets for environmental goods by replacing missing price incentives with administered taxes or charges. For example, governments can develop a system of natural resource taxes for forestry, fisheries, and water that provide incentives for more sustainable extraction and effective tax collection and monitoring schemes to enforce. In theory, some instruments are better for reducing incentives for over-extraction (e.g., taxes on the volume of extraction), but these can be costly to administer as they also provide incentives for tax evasion. Considering the transaction cost of policy implementation, simpler taxes, such as traded exports and/or audited profits, may be preferred.

(iii) **Payments for environmental services.** This is a policy instrument that can be used to provide compensation for additional environmental services provided by food system actors. For example, payment for environmental services can be designed to compensate for the environmental services that forests offer, such as carbon sequestration, watershed protection, or biodiversity conservation. The PRC has conducted numerous national, provincial, and local experiments over the past decade in environmental policy tools under the broad heading of ecocompensation, focusing mostly on water resources management (Box 4).

(iv) **Environmental markets.** Tradable permits for regulating environmental externalities can often achieve environmental targets at a lower cost than environmental tax and payment for environmental services. This is because trading allows a cost-effective allocation of environmental effort across alternative sources without environmental regulators knowing the abatement costs of individual agents (OECD 2010). Creating a market for pollution quota, such as manure trading in the Netherlands, results in a price tag for the polluting substances and induces polluters to seek ways to reduce costs (OECD 2010). The most visible developments internationally are those which address GHGs (e.g., carbon trading). Another growing area is water quality trading, including programs to address agricultural sources of water pollution.

(v) **Valuation of natural capital and its ecosystem services.** The monetary value of natural capital stocks and ecosystem services is fundamental information for policy makers to design policy programs and channel investments to where capital creates the most social and environmental value. Such active initiatives already exist in the agrifood sector and in other industry sectors.[9] One concrete action is the development of sustainability guidelines for investors and integrated profit and loss reporting frameworks— either as mandated by regulation or simply as generally accepted accounting principles by the industry—that play a critical role in communicating natural, social, and financial value to investors (Millan, Limketkai, and Guarnaschelli 2019). Collecting integrated profit and loss reporting data and information, as well as climate outcome metrics, to better understand the environmental and social impact of sustainable investments and their underlying financial benefits (e.g., improved productivity, cost savings, reduced risks) will help convince a broader pool of mainstream and/or institutional investors of the value creation of sustainable and/or climate-oriented practices.

(vi) **Traceability and ecolabeling.** For market prices to integrate the true costs of producing and distributing food, consumers need to have better information

---

[9] The Economics of Ecosystems and Biodiversity initiative of the United Nations Environment Programme published the Scientific and Economic Foundations Report for the agrifood sector. The Natural Capital Coalition is a network where leading initiatives and organizations have agreed on a generally accepted framework—the Natural Capital Protocol—on how to value natural capital (including sector guidance for food and beverage). Another important progress in recent years has been made with the United Nations System of Environmental Economic Accounting–Ecosystem Accounting (Hein, Bagstad, and Obst 2020) as the leading analytical framework to measure the state and use of ecosystem capital (including ecosystem services). A detailed methodological framework is available including for valuing natural capital and externalities, and the system has been tested in over 30 countries worldwide, including India, Indonesia, Japan, the PRC, and the Philippines.

on the relationship between their activities, the subsequent natural capital impacts, and their dependencies on natural capital. Informing consumers of the environmental and health implications of their food choices can drive food system transformation from the demand side. Ecolabeling and environmental standards should be applied to facilitate consumers' informed choices. Digitalization of food supply chains is allowing the traceability of the origin of food. Consumers' collective purchasing power, and its influence on food-industry priorities, has the potential to stimulate market growth and be a powerful force to drive food system transformation.

Box 4: Development of Ecocompensation Schemes in the People's Republic of China

Ecocompensation schemes in the People's Republic of China (PRC) generally consist of negotiated contractual arrangements between those who provide and those who benefit from ecosystem services, with payments conditional on the protection and delivery of targeted services. Ecocompensation has gradually progressed to embody three key policy directions for environmental management reform in the PRC: (i) experimentation in the use of policy instruments (e.g., payments for ecosystem services); (ii) promotion of more integrated, intersectoral, and interregional management frameworks; and (iii) expansion and diversification of funding sources via more direct engagement of a wider range of key stakeholders and economic actors.

The PRC has experimented with different ecocompensation schemes, including national experiments in water pollution emission permits trading, local and provincial experiments in water-use rights trading, provincial programs that create a system of penalties or rewards that are transferred between administrative sections of rivers based on water pollution targets, and programs providing downstream development concessions to upstream governments to offset losses associated with upstream development restrictions created to protect important drinking water source areas. In 2011, the pilot cross-provincial ecocompensation scheme between Zhejiang and Anhui provinces established an upstream–downstream financial transfer arrangement. This national pilot ecocompensation scheme contributed to reducing traditional pollutants (e.g., chemical oxygen demand) from manufacturing and industries. The water quality at the interprovincial section has met the standards agreed between the two provinces, and the water quality of Xin'an River went higher than the national average.

Source: Asian Development Bank.

Scaling Up Private Investment in Food System Transformation

Private investment is key to closing the financing gap to food system transformation. Subsidy and grant programs act as a push mechanism to initiate the transformation to resilient and sustainable food systems, but they are not sufficient in size or catalytic impact. Countries and donor agencies also face constraints to increase public investment in food system transformation as they are under intensive pressure to spend for short-term mitigation measures in the recovery from the COVID-19 pandemic. Private sector interventions play a critical role in closing the funding gaps for food system transformations. However, the availability of investable business models and large-scale bankable projects are limited. Early-stage business models with long development lead times and technical assistance requirements, and uncertain financial and/or environmental upside—particularly within the smallholder farmer context in developing countries—reduce investor appetite for opportunities outside of business-as-usual agriculture and forestry investments (Millan, Limketkai, and Guarnaschelli 2019). Developing an enabling environment is essential to accurately assess risk and deploy appropriate risk-mitigating mechanisms, as well as equip investors with data and risk tools necessary to execute better risk assessment and management strategies. Addressing key barriers would unlock private sector financing from farmers, food and agriculture companies, domestic and international financial institutions, and specialized investors (World Bank 2018).

Transitional finance is required to address the multiyear gap between investments and financial benefits. Actions to transform food systems are often considered medium- to long-term investments that do not generate financial benefits in the short term, which create a maturity mismatch between investments and financial benefits. For example, sustainable agricultural production practices such as conservation tillage, cover crops, and extended crop rotations all have different costs and benefits over time. Some practices entail upfront and/or ongoing costs for seed and new equipment. This transition often takes a few years and can involve a temporary drop in yields and income as the farmer takes time to learn and the soil takes time to adapt.[10] Transition financing involves the use of loans wherein repayment terms are pushed back to accommodate multiyear return gaps associated with transitioning to new practices (Millan, Limketkai, and Guarnaschelli 2019). In the United States, transitional finance mechanisms are tested in the shift to organic production, which supports environmental quality and improves farm profit. Those funds usually offer 3-year operating loans to farmers transitioning to organic production, with market off-take support and repayment over 8 to 10 years through a 10%–50% revenue share (EDF 2020).

---

[10]   Research by the EDF and others shows that the upfront costs associated with these practices are typically offset within this 3- to 5-year time frame by savings in production costs, crop yield improvements, or resilience, and in some cases new forms of farm revenue (Monast, Sands, and Grafton 2018; Sustainable Agriculture and Education 2019; Precision Conservation Management 2019).

Blended finance can leverage private sector investment in food system transformation. Blended finance is a structuring approach that allows different types of capital, whether public, impact, or commercially oriented, to invest alongside each other while each achieves its own objectives (Convergence 2021). It has various forms including risk mitigation mechanisms (e.g., guarantees, insurance); direct funding (e.g., equity, debts, or grants); indirect funding (onlending by public financial institutions) or results-based incentives (e.g., performance-based contracts). Public or private capital in blended finance applications is primarily used to take higher risks in projects (e.g., through "first loss" or repayment guarantees; OECD 2021). Blended finance structures are typically used in circumstances where there are perceived or real risks by private investors, and where public capital can take more risk (without the commensurate return expectations) to catalyze investments faster (OECD 2021). Catalytic capital from public sources can play an important role in increasing the pace of investment in sustainable agriculture by addressing prevailing barriers and enabling the proliferation of new financial models (EDF 2020). It facilitates the flow of commercial capital to enterprises and projects that have an explicit impact objective by filling the gap between a project's original risk–return profile and the

---

Box 5: The Case of the Global Agriculture and Food Security Program

The Global Agriculture and Food Security Program (GAFSP) is a demand-led and recipient-owned global partnership and a cost-effective and flexible multilateral financing mechanism focused on achieving Sustainable Development Goal 2: ending hunger, poverty, and malnutrition in developing countries. GAFSP brings together a range of agricultural development stakeholders, including farmer organizations, civil society organizations, donors, and recipients, to prioritize programming and allocate funds. Investments are made in three broad areas: strengthening service providers, strengthening core value-chain actors, and improving the enabling environment.

An example of blended finance is the program's private sector window where the International Finance Corporation uses concessional funds from the GAFSP Private Sector Window alongside its own commercial funding—to support projects that are not commercially attractive due to the high risk involved. These mechanisms allow GAFSP to crowd in additional investment—$5.30 of private financing for every $1 of public or donor capital invested—which in turn allows the fund to provide affordable financing with fewer requirements for riskier projects. That same window provides technical and financing advisory services to improve operations, productivity, and standards as well as to uncover financing opportunities and create markets. To date, the private sector window has invested $311 million in 61 investment projects aimed at benefitting small and medium-sized enterprises and smallholder farmers around the world.

Source: GAFSP. 2019. *Changing Lives: Private Sector Solutions for Helping Small Farmers.* Washington, DC.

requirements of market-rate investors (Box 5). Many investment funds are scaling up co-investment with the public sector such as Althelia Climate Fund II and Land Degradation Neutrality Fund by Mirova Natural Capital, AGRI3 by Rabobank, Tropical Landscape Finance Facility by ADM Capital, and BNP Paribas (Millan, Limketkai, and Guarnaschelli 2019).

Channeling green finance to food system transformation. Green financing is a financial flow from the public, private, and not-for-profit sectors to sustainable development priorities (United Nations Environment Programme 2019). While a number of climate commitments include agriculture in their mitigation targets or reference agriculture as an adaptation priority, the total amount of climate finance allocated to agriculture, forestry, and other land use was disproportionally small (World Bank 2016).[11] Green finance allows smallholder farmers and small and medium-sized enterprises (SMEs) to fund investments in food system transformation such as low-emission, climate-resilient, and sustainable agriculture. However, high transaction costs and small ticket sizes pose significant barriers for commercially oriented investors to invest. The development of climate valuation methodologies as well as simpler and standardized products can make green finance in food systems as an investable asset class for investors. Aggregation and securitization will also be key to converting investment products into marketable securities that are available to a wider pool of investors with different risk–return appetites. Deal matchmaking platforms are needed to facilitate transactions between a pipeline of investable projects and pools of investment capital (Millan, Limketkai, and Guarnaschelli 2019). Another approach to mobilizing greater private capital for climate adaptation projects is through investment vehicles such as social, green, and resilience funds (World Bank 2021). For example, social impact bonds and other sustainability-linked debt products can provide a lower lending rate or pricing reward for sustainability or environment, social, and governance performance. The market for green funds has also been growing, although currently it does not have a unified definition (Munoz, Vargas, and Marco 2014; Voica, Panait, and Radulescu 2015; Yuan 2017).

Structuring financial instruments can connect different pools of capital to food system transformation. Most of the actors in food systems are dominated by SMEs, including primary producers. Most of the more than 400 million farmers in Asia are small holders, while 90% of food processors are SMEs (Fan et al. 2021). They are typically at a disadvantage with respect to large firms when accessing finance, owing to opacity, under-collateralization, high transaction costs, and lack of financial skills. Bank credit plays a dominant role in providing external capital to SMEs, but alternative financing tools, such as equity finance, corporate bonds issuance, and mezzanine finance are generally underutilized by SMEs. The formation of special funds initiated by the public sector has contributed to filling the gap in equity needs (Koreen and Nemoto 2019). ADB's Anhui Huangshan Xin'an River Ecological Protection and Green Development Project in the PRC provides a model of the structured green investment fund to support SMEs involved in green business that suffer from lack of access to long-term financing because of the general perception

---

[11] Climate finance is a subset of green finance and refers to the flows of capital from both public and private sources to achieve climate change adaptation and mitigation objectives.

of low financial returns from their investments in ecological agriculture, ecotourism, and pollution control (Box 6).

Leveraging Innovations in Digital Technologies for Food System Transformation

Digital technologies can improve the productivity of entire food supply chains and offer new financial tools. Digital technologies provide tools to collect, store, analyze, and share information digitally. Data-driven innovations can reduce transaction costs by increasing efficiency and transparency (De Clercq, Vats, and Biel 2018). At the production stage, big data analytics, internet of things, and sensors help farmers' decision-making through accurate, timely, and location-specific price, weather, and agronomic data and information. They also facilitate the acquisition of skills

---

Box 6: Innovative Green Finance Mechanism: Anhui Huangshan Xin'an River Ecological Protection and Green Development Project in the People's Republic of China

The Asian Development Bank (ADB) is piloting innovative green finance mechanisms in the People's Republic of China to reduce rural pollution and support the development of sustainable agriculture. Working with Huangshan Municipal Government, ADB developed an ecocompensation and green incentive and investment fund mechanism consisting of Cross-Provincial Ecocompensation Green Investment Fund (GIF) and the Huangshan Tea Farmer Green Incentive Mechanism (GIM). This dual pooled fund arrangement is designed to improve the sustainability of the ongoing ecocompensation scheme, given that the revenue generated from GIF can be used to provide cash grants under the ecocompensation scheme.

GIF is financed from the compensation payments which the Huangshan Municipal Government received from the Xin'an River Eco-compensation Scheme between Anhui and Zhejiang provinces. GIF invests primarily in pollution control measures, including wastewater treatment facilities and related infrastructure. On the other hand, GIM provides direct payments to tea farmers to encourage them to adopt environmentally sustainable farming and farm management practices (e.g., integrated pest management, slope stability, water conservation, and drainage improvement), thus effectively reducing agricultural nonpoint source pollution. GIM will be introduced on a pilot basis under the project funded by ADB and KfW Bank. GIM can offer a self-financing mechanism for ecocompensation by promoting commercial financing and reducing the fiscal burden on central and local governments' budgets. A wider adoption of sustainable production practices could demonstrate associated economic benefits from organic certification of tea products and green production processes.

Source: Asian Development Bank.

and knowledge and improve the efficiency of capital input such as machinery and equipment. At the distribution stage, conventional food supply chains comprise many transactions in the agrifood subsectors, including wholesalers and intermediaries for commodities, equipment, and processed goods. These transactions generate costs as every additional player demands a share of profits and every additional transaction increases the risk of fraud (European Investment Bank 2019). Digital technologies can reduce the transaction costs and improve product traceability and integrity, contract certainty, proof and/or verification of geographic origin, and compliance with sanitary and phytosanitary requirements. In addition, digital technologies offer new financial tools by enabling digital payments and creating digital footprints to build credit profiles.

Digital transformation of food supply chains is generating new business models to accelerate sustainable and resilient food system transformation. The COVID-19 pandemic accelerated a digital transformation of food systems. Development of agricultural e-commerce is modernizing food supply chains and represents new investment opportunities as innovative digital start-ups focused on transforming food systems are emerging in Asia (Box 7). In the PRC, e-commerce has emerged as a critical force during the COVID-19 pandemic in ensuring the delivery of food to urban residents in the face of strict prevention and control measures through matching agricultural producers, input suppliers, and marketing companies, and providing logistical support (Zhan and Chen 2021). Relatively well-served road infrastructure, access to internet and mobile phones, and well-developed supply chains contributed to relatively stable food supply in Asia during the COVID-19 pandemic (Fan et al. 2021). Beyond enhancing market connectivity and value chain development, digital technologies are making food supply chains more demand-driven by helping to overcome information gaps and asymmetries between producers and consumers, allowing stakeholders with different preferences and incentives to work better together. Digital technologies are also offering new business models to support food system transformation through offering innovations in food supply chains.

(i) **Climate change mitigation and adaptation.** Sensor technologies, big data analytics, and blockchain technologies are increasingly being used to monitor and analyze climatic conditions and initiate mitigation measures. Applications include automated early warning systems for crop or livestock health, weather, pests, and diseases that can facilitate proactive and timely management responses. It is estimated that the adoption of precision agriculture technologies such as on-farm sensors, remote sensing, internet of things, and big data analytics by 15%–25% of the farm population could reduce annual GHG emissions by 5–20 megatons, water use by 50 billion–180 billion cubic meters, and the cost of production by $40 billion–$100 billion globally by 2030 (World Economic Forum 2018).

(ii) **Sustainable use of natural resources.** The demand-driven food supply chains facilitated by digitalization can make the environmental and climate footprint in the food supply chain transparent to consumers. Armed with information through appropriate labeling and traceability systems, consumers' choices could thus reflect the implicit value of environmental and biodiversity impacts. Remote sensing, spectral analysis, and blockchain can effectively reduce GHG emissions and water use. Information technology-based, farm-, or estate-level natural capital accounts showing farming externalities, dependencies, and impacts on ecosystems and the services they supply have been developed and are being tested to inform farmers of the effects of farm management on natural capital. It is being examined how these can be aggregated to inform on overall environmental performance of the farming sector, and if and how specific indicators extracted from these accounts can be linked to information systems of banks, allowing them to better monitor the environmental impacts of their lending portfolio and potentially rewarding farmers with better environmental performance.

(iii) **Reducing food loss and waste.** Poor farming practices, lack of good postharvest management, inefficient processing and supply chains, and lack of awareness at the retail and/or consumer level are some of the major issues that cause food loss and waste. Mobile phone-based extension can help farmers in developing countries gain knowledge and receive advisory services from agriculture experts. Artificial intelligence and big data can help farmers diagnose pests in real time and take necessary actions to minimize crop loss. Digital technologies such as artificial intelligence and machine learning are used by leading retailers in Europe to introduce "dynamic discounting" to motivate consumers to buy near expiry foods at discounted prices, thereby significantly reducing food loss at the retail level.

Digital infrastructure should be developed to reduce the digital divide. Although digital technologies improve efficiency and transparency of food value chains, they may also limit competition and, under certain conditions, encourage greater collusion among companies (World Bank 2019). Privacy and data issues in digital agriculture can erode people's trust in technologies. As in all sectors of the economy, there is a need for transparency and clarity around issues such as data ownership, portability, privacy, trust, and liability (FAO 2020c). The introduction of robotics and artificial intelligence could be beneficial in agricultural sectors that are characterized by a low supply of workers (FAO 2020c), but it may cause workforce displacement. The availability of digital skills and digital infrastructure such as broadband internet access may increase the inequality. This can create problems in rural areas where the human capital and physical infrastructure needed to exploit the positive potential of digitalization are lacking. Addressing these concerns calls for policies to keep service provider entry barriers low; ensure good data governance; foster inclusion through targeted support to smallholder farmers, youth, women, and other vulnerable groups; and support skills development.

Box 7: Development of Agriculture E-commerce in the People's Republic of China

The recent development of agriculture e-commerce in the People's Republic of China (PRC) can be categorized into three models. The first model involves nationwide e-commerce platforms that represent a major channel for online sales of fresh agricultural products to consumers with a wide market scope and a large transaction volume. The platforms offer a full range of agricultural products suitable for long-distance transportation. However, due to the low entry barrier for merchants and fierce competition, price remains the main means of competition. The second model involves local governments that organize agriculture e-commerce using third-party platforms. In this model, merchants are required to obtain government permission to enter the platform to guarantees the quality of agricultural products. The third model is done through unofficial channels based on social network platforms.

The traditional vegetables supply chains in the PRC have many inefficiencies. Every intermediary link, such as producers, farmers' brokers, wholesale markets in production areas, wholesale markets in sales areas, and vendors in the vegetable market, incurs costs that eventually increase the prices of food products. Farmers often produce without effectively capturing demand information because of the information asymmetry in the traditional vegetable supply chain. Farmers' brokers also suffer from the unstable supply of vegetables and the fluctuating purchasing prices set by wholesalers. The wholesalers and vegetable vendors bear the logistics expenses in addition to the booth entry fee to the wholesale markets.

Songxiaocai Company, a business-to-business trading platform for vegetables, developed an innovative information and communication technology solution to improve the inefficiency in the traditional vegetable supply chain and stablish demand-driven supply chains. Songxiaocai positioned itself as a one-stop intermediary. Based on the demand of the final customers, small vendors and wholesalers can place orders specifying the variety, category, grade, price, quantity, and origin of production through the mobile applications maintained by Songxiaocai. The orders from vendors and wholesalers allow producers to prepare the deliverables to meet the specified demand. The standardized products are packaged and transported directly to the end customers, thus reducing the lead time for additional dismantling and sorting in the supply chain and improving product quality. Through Songxiaocai, vendors in the same area might order products from the same supplier. With the pooling of all of the orders, these vendors can enjoy advantages in competitive price, and stable supply of quality products.

Sources: Yao et al. (2019), Guo et al. (2020).

Implications for ADB's Engagement with Sustainable and Resilient Food Systems

ADB's intervention should be designed to provide holistic solutions covering entire food supply chains. Increased investments in agriculture, natural resources, and rural development over four times in the last decade, from $1.6 billion in 2009–2011 to $6 billion in 2018–2020. ADB continues to diversify its portfolio away from agriculture production infrastructure. Moving forward, ADB is well-positioned to support food system transformation in Asia and the Pacific, leveraging on private and public partnerships, and providing innovative knowledge solutions. ADB 's intervention can benefit from more holistic design covering food supply chains (Figure 2). For example, promoting sustainable agricultural production and regenerating farming can be supported by the traceability or certification system along food supply chains that allow downstream consumers to compensate the additional costs associated with such farming practices. Building more resilient food supply chains requires investments in strengthening logistics and storage networks, improving access to financial services among SMEs and farmers, and developing price monitoring systems along food supply chains. Promotion of healthy and nutritious diets requires interventions both at the production and demand sides.

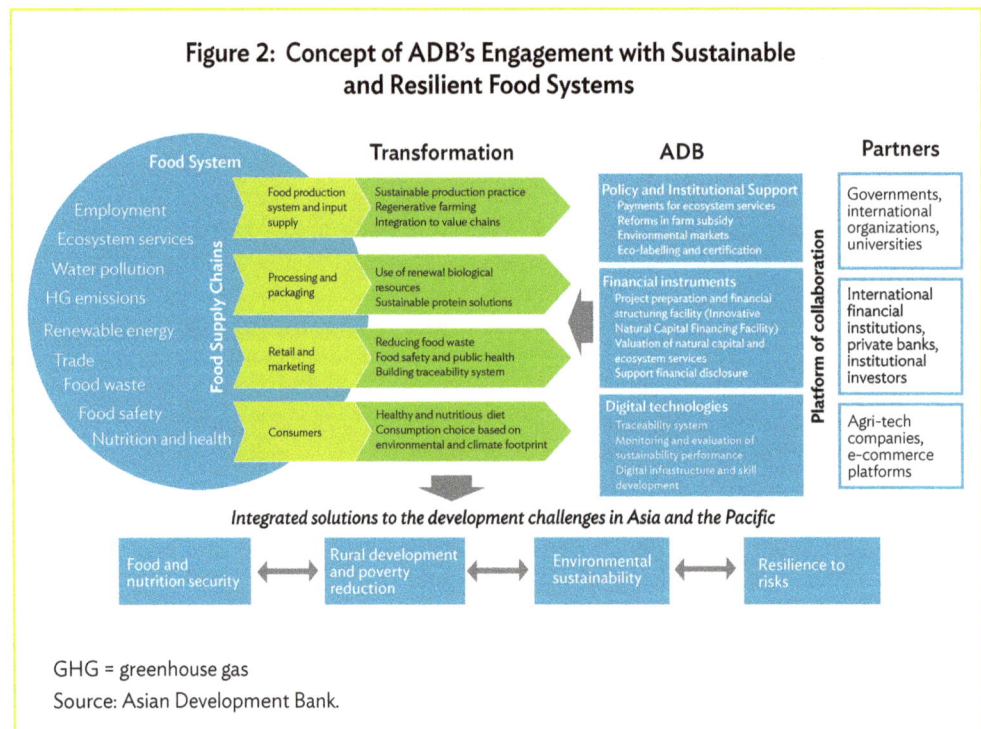

Figure 2: Concept of ADB's Engagement with Sustainable and Resilient Food Systems

GHG = greenhouse gas

Source: Asian Development Bank.

Support enabling policy and institutional environment for food system transformation. Food system transformation requires joint actions by all stakeholders including national and local governments, food system actors, and international donor agencies. ADB can support the development of policies and institutions that provide the right incentives to minimize environmental and health consequences. For example, ADB's Natural Capital Lab initiative is a virtual and living platform to share knowledge, build partnerships, and serve as a testbed for mobilizing public and private investments in natural capital and green business development. Natural Capital Lab can be a hub to share institutional and regulatory frameworks that address environmental degradation and contribute to food system sustainability, such as payment for environmental services, emission trading schemes, and ecolabels. ADB can use existing tools and innovative technologies in the lab for capturing the value of ecosystems as assets (i.e., forests, watershed, and landscape valuation) to mainstream nature-positive solutions to influence decision-making processes.

Provide financial instruments to unlock private investment in sustainable and resilient food systems. Scaling up private investment plays a key role in closing the large funding gap for sustainable and resilient food system transformation. ADB can provide catalytic capital and financial instruments to leverage private finance for the sustainability and resilience goals of food systems. Blended finance offers an opportunity to prove the financial viability of investments in sustainable and resilient food systems to private investors and commercial lenders. Farmers and SME entrepreneurs represent a large share of operators in the food systems and are particularly disadvantaged in accessing finance. ADB can enhance financial delivery channels for food system transformation by SMEs and smallholder farmers. For example, formation of intermediary investment funds can support SMEs involved in green business such as ecological agriculture, ecotourism, and pollution control that are suffering from lack of access to long-term financing. Financial instruments such as aggregation and securitization can make investment in sustainable and resilient food systems to investable products and channel funding from a wider pool of investors with different risk–return appetites.

Facilitate the application of digital technologies. Digital technology is generating new businesses and financial models that can help accelerate food system transformation. Digital transformation is increasing the efficiency of food supply chains and providing a breakthrough to existing barriers to the sustainable and resilient food system transformation. Digital technologies provide tools to monitor and evaluate the sustainability performance of food supply chains, which create new financing channels including consumers to compensate for the implicit cost of natural capital and ecosystem services. For example, remote sensing, spectral analysis, and blockchain technology can effectively reduce GHG emissions and water use, among other benefits. Digital technologies are also offering new financial tools by enabling digital payments and creating digital footprints to build credit profiles. ADB should proactively use its knowledge capacity and financial instruments to support progress in these areas in collaboration with development partners, including the private sector. ADB's interventions can have demonstrative effects in adopting digital solutions to food system transformation. ADB should also play a role in reducing the

Figure 3: Concept of ADB's Innovative Natural Capital Financing Facility

Natural Capital Fund

Co-finance projects secured against future increment income and ecocompensation

Natural Capital Lab

Build valuation tools, knowledge and best practices; training for better utilization; policy and regulation

Innovative Natural Capital Financing Facility

Agribusiness Service Platform

Digitize supply chains to help project sponsors improve and upgrade value creation in marketing, procurement, and logistics

Source: Asian Development Bank.

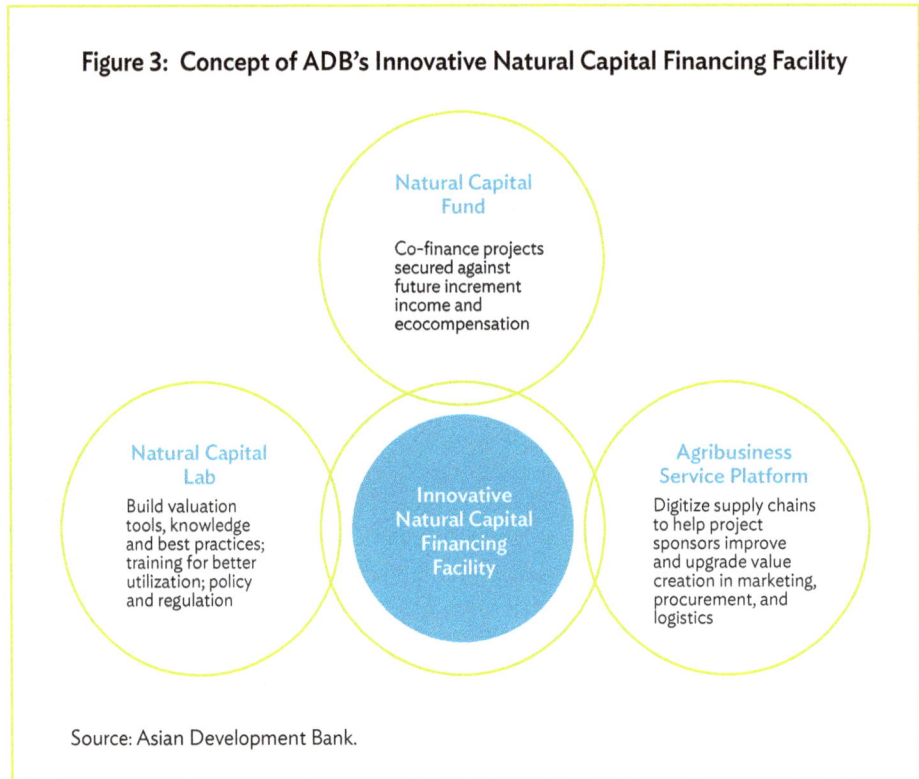

digital divide in rural areas as the lack of digital infrastructure and skills to access these technologies increases inequalities.

Establish a multistakeholder platform for food system transformation. Transformative changes in food systems require joint actions among international, national, and local agencies, knowledge institutes, nongovernment organizations, the private sector, and communities in Asia and the Pacific. ADB can play an important role in facilitating the exchange of financial and knowledge solutions in the region collaborating with multiple stakeholders. This platform can facilitate south–south cooperation, as well as triangular cooperation, among developing and developed countries, providing knowledge and assessment, capacity building, and policy services for promoting best practice in developing sustainable and resilient food systems in the region.

Establish a financial facility to support ADB's project preparation and financial structuring to support food system transformation. ADB can establish a dedicated financial facility to prepare investment projects on sustainable and resilient food systems with governments and other food system actors. More specifically, the facility can support the identification of possible sources of public and private funding and develop the financial structures and operational designs to mobilize the expected resources and implement such projects with economic, social, and environmental sustainability. The facility can also support the monitoring and evaluation of the implemented projects. An innovative natural capital financing facility can be composed of three pillars—a natural capital lab, an agribusiness service platform, and a natural capital fund. An innovative natural capital financing facility can comprehensively support ADB's engagement in food system transformation and develop robust investable pipelines (Figure 3). While the natural capital lab functions as a hub to share knowledge on enabling a policy and institutional environment for food system transformation, the natural capital fund functions as a financial facility to support project preparation and financial structuring to scale up ADB's catalytic investment in sustainable and resilient food system transformation. The agribusiness service platform is designed to support ADB projects in applying digital technologies to improve the resilience and sustainability of food supply chains in partnership with the private sector.

References

Asian Development Bank (ADB). 2020. An Updated Assessment of the Potential Economic Impact of COVID-19. *ADB Briefs*. No. 133. Manila.

Centre for Research on the Epidemiology of Disasters. 2017. EM-DAT: International Disaster database. Centre for Research on the Epidemiology of Disasters (accessed 17 May 2021).

Convergence. 2021. Blended Finance Primer (accessed 5 July 2021).

De Clercq, M., A. Vats, and A. Biel. 2018. *Agriculture 4.0 – The Future of Farming Technology*. In collaboration with Oliver Wyman.

European Investment Bank. 2019. Feeding future generations How finance can boost innovation in agri-food.

Environmental Defense Fund. 2020. *Catalytic Capital and Agriculture Opportunities to Invest in Healthy Soils, Resilient Farms and a Stable Climate*.

European Commission. 2018. *A Sustainable Bioeconomy for Europe: Strengthening the Connection Between Economy, Society and the Environment – Updated Bioeconomy Strategy*.

Fan, S., et al. 2021. *Food System Resilience and COVID-19 – Lessons from the Asian Experience*. Global Food Security. 28.

Food and Agriculture Organization of the United Nations (FAO)–UN Environment. 2014. *Agri-Food Task Force on Sustainable Consumption and Production*. Fifth Meeting. Summary Report.

FAO. 2011. Global Food Losses and Food Waste – Extent, Causes and Prevention.

———. 2017. *Save Food for a Better Climate: Converting the Food Loss and Waste Challenge into Climate Action*.

———. 2019. *The State of Food Security and Nutrition in the World*.

———. 2020a. *Building Sustainable and Resilient Food Systems in Asia and the Pacific*.

———. 2020b. *Circular Economy: Waste-to-Resource & COVID-19*.

———. 2020c. *FAO Regional Conference for Asia and the Pacific. 35th Session Digitalization of Food and Agriculture*.

FAO, International Fund for Agricultural Development, and World Food Programme. 2015. *Achieving Zero Hunger: The Critical Role of Investments in Social Protection and Agriculture*.

FAO et al. 2019. *Placing Nutrition at the Centre of Social Protection. Asia and the Pacific Regional Overview of Food Security and Nutrition 2019*. Bangkok: FAO.

FAO et al. 2021. *Maternal and Child Diets at the Heart of Improving Nutrition. Asia and the Pacific Regional Overview of Food Security and Nutrition 2020*. Bangkok: FAO.

Food and Land Use Coalition. 2019. *Global Consultation Report of the Food and Land Use Coalition. Growing Better: Ten Critical Transitions to Transform Food and Land Use*.

Guo, H., et al. 2020. The Role of e-Commerce in the Urban Food System Under COVID-19: Lessons from China. *China Agricultural Economic Review*.

Hein, L. et al. 2020. Progress in Natural Capital Accounting for Ecosystems. *Science*. 367 (6477). pp. 514–515.

Herrero, M. et al. 2013. *Biomass Use, Production, Feed Efficiencies, and Greenhouse Gas Emissions from Global Livestock Systems.* Proceedings of the National Academy of Sciences. 110 (52). pp. 20888-20893.

Intergovernmental Science-Policy Platform on Biodiversity and Ecosystem Services. 2019. Summary for policymakers of the regional assessment report on biodiversity and ecosystem services for Asia and the Pacific of the Intergovernmental Science-Policy Platform on Biodiversity and Ecosystem Services.

Intergovernmental Panel on Climate Change (IPCC). 2020. *An IPCC Special Report on Climate Change, Desertification, Land Degradation, Sustainable Land Management, Food Security, and Greenhouse Gas Fluxes in Terrestrial Ecosystems*.

Koreen, N., and M. Nemoto. 2019. *Digital Innovation Can Improve Financial Access for SMEs*.

McKinsey Global Institute. 2014. *Overcoming Obesity: An Initial Economic Analysis*.

Millan A., B. Limketkai, and S. Guarnaschelli. 2019. *Financing the Transformation of Food Systems Under a Changing Climate*. CCAFS Report. Wageningen, the Netherlands: CGIAR Research Program on Climate Change, Agriculture and Food Security (CCAFS).

Monast, M., L. Sands, and A. Grafton. 2018. *Farm Finance and Conservation: How Stewardship Generates Value for Farmers, Lenders, Insurers and Landowners*.

Munoz, F., Vargas, M., and I. Marco. 2014. Environmental Mutual Funds: Financial Performance and Managerial Abilities. *Journal of Business Ethics*. 124 (4). pp. 551–569.

Organisation for Economic Co-operation and Development (OECD). 2010. *Guidelines for Cost-Effective Agri-Environmental Policy Measures*. Paris: OECD Publishing.

———. 2019. *Accelerating Climate Action: Refocusing Policies Through a Well-being Lens.* Paris: OECD Publishing.

———. 2020a. *Strengthening Agricultural Resilience in the Face of Multiple Risks*, Paris: OECD Publishing.

———. 2020b. *Agricultural Policy Monitoring and Evaluation 2020*. Paris: OECD Publishing.

———. 2021. *The OECD DAC Blended Finance Guidance*. Paris: OECD Publishing.

Precision Conservation Management. 2019. *The Business Case for Conservation: Cost-Benefit Analysis of Conservation Practices*.

Scherr, S. J., A. White, and D. Kaimowitz. 2004. *A New Agenda for Forest Conservation and Poverty Reduction*.

Sustainable Agriculture and Education. 2019. *Cover Crop Economics: Opportunities to Improve Your Bottom Line in Row Crops*.

United Nations Economic and Social Commission for Asia and the Pacific. 2020. *Policy Brief: Sustainable Food Systems and Nutrition Health Dietary Patterns*.

United Nations Environment Programme. 2019. *Driving Finance Today for the Climate Resilient Society of Tomorrow*.

Voica, M. C., Panait, M. and Radulescu, I. 2015. Green Investments—Between Necessity, Fiscal Constraints and Profit. *Procedia Economics & Finance*. 22. pp. 72–79.

World Health Organization. 2015. *Cancer: Carcinogenicity of the Consumption of Red Meat and Processed Meat*.

World Bank. 2016. *Making Climate Finance Work in Agriculture*. Washington, D.C.

———. 2018. *Future of Food: Maximizing Finance for Development in Agricultural Value Chains*.

———. 2019. *Future of Food: Harnessing Digital Technologies to Improve Food System Outcomes*.

———. 2021. *Enabling Private Investment in Climate Adaptation and Resilience: Current Status, Barriers to Investment and Blueprint for Action*.

World Economic Forum. 2018. *Innovation with a Purpose: The Role of Technology Innovation in Accelerating Food Systems Transformation*.

Yao, Y. et al. 2019. How to Become a System Integrator Streamlining Vegetable Supply Chains: The Case of Songxiaocai Company. *International Food and Agribusiness Management Review*. 22 (4). pp. 621–634.

Yuan, Y. 2017. Environmental Performance and Financial Performance of Green Mutual Fund—Evidence from China. *Open Journal of Business and Management*. 5 (4). pp. 680–698.

Zhan, Y. and K. Chen. 2021. Building Resilient Food Systems Amidst COVID-19: Responses and Lessons from China. *Agricultural Systems*. 190 (May). pp. 1–7.

www.ingramcontent.com/pod-product-compliance
Lightning Source LLC
Chambersburg PA
CBHW050058220326
41599CB00045B/7455